T0392282

PRAYER
THE SUPREME WEAPON

A Prayer Guide for Christian Women

by
Lurene Emanuel

WESTBOW
PRESS®
A DIVISION OF THOMAS NELSON
& ZONDERVAN

WestBow Press books may be ordered through booksellers or by contacting:

WestBow Press
A Division of Thomas Nelson & Zondervan
1663 Liberty Drive
Bloomington, IN 47403
www.westbowpress.com
844-714-3454

Scripture quotations are taken from the King James Version of the Bible.

ISBN: 979-8-3850-2122-2 (sc)
ISBN: 979-8-3850-2123-9 (e)

Library of Congress Control Number: 2024905254

Print information available on the last page.

WestBow Press rev. date: 09/27/2024

This book is dedicated in memory of several people who have been very important in my life.
Their influence and love have served as a source of strength and inspiration.

Reverend B. F. Dudley Sr. ~ Grandfather
Annie L. Fisher ~ Mother
Alice M. Anderson ~ Spiritual Mother and Prayer Warrior
Mother Marie Kilpatrick ~ Prayer Warrior Lamarius Cox ~ Prayer Partner

PRAYER THE SUPREME WEAPON

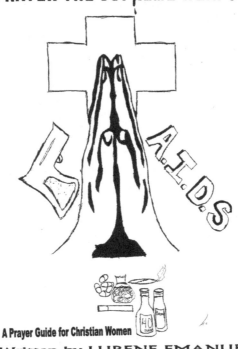

A Prayer Guide for Christian Women

Written by LURENE EMANUEL

TABLE OF CONTENTS

ACKNOWLEDGEMENTS

It is in the honor and presence of God that I acknowledge the outpouring of his anointing power, which has allowed me to compile these inspirational thoughts in the form of a book.

It is with grateful appreciation that I thank my Prayer Warriors: Ariel S. Dudley; my grandmother, Lecy Lindsey; and Nell Montgomery and Hattie Square, my Spiritual Mothers, for their constant prayers, concern, and guidance.

I salute my Sisters in Christ: Edna Andry and Barbara Bolden, for their encouragement and critiques; and Mother Carrie Judge of the Florida State Convention, for her confidence in my teaching endeavors.

No ministry or accomplishment can be happily achieved without the support of one's family. I thank my heavenly Father for blessing me with a wonderful family. Thanks to my husband and spiritual leader, Elder Robert J. Emanuel Jr., for his editing of the scriptural references; my daughter Lenice, for editing and formatting the texts, as well as her love and support; and my daughter Letariel and sons Robert III (Jerome) and Benjamin, for their encouragement and faith in me.

Finally, thank you to the visual illustrators, Kendal, and Quinton Smith, along with their parents, John and Cynthia Smith, for allowing me the opportunity to use their talents.

May God continue to richly bless each of you in all that you do!

FOREWORD

Lenice C. Emanuel, MLA,
Daughter of Lurene Fisher Emanuel, MS, author of
"Prayer the Supreme Weapon"

When my mother asked me to write the foreword for her book, "Prayer the Supreme Weapon," which is a prayer guide for Christian women, not only was I honored, but I was inspired to think about the subject of prayer more deeply. I thought about how prayer is defined, how I have observed the power of prayer in my mother's life, and, more personally, what prayer has meant in my own life, especially as a woman. A simple concept in theory, prayer is generally defined as a conversation between an individual and God. Given that premise, in hindsight, I have thought it both neglectful and humorous when I consider the number of times I have fallen asleep while praying or never actually finished a prayer because of a distraction. And, let us be honest, in today's fast paced society, distractions are more pronounced than ever. We have access to more information in the history of time, and with minimal effort, yet we seemingly have less knowledge and wisdom. In fact, our attention spans are so limited that researchers have stated that if one does not capture the attention of a reader or viewer within nine seconds, the average person's attention will likely not be held. In transparency, I must admit, I am the "average" person. Yet, the God of all creation is patient and incredibly tolerate of us and all of our weaknesses, including our often-limited attention span when it comes to our "conversations" with Him. In this way, my mother's book, "Prayer, the Supreme Weapon," is an incredible tool, not only regarding how to pray, but how prayer has manifested in the lives of others, particularly women. As both a woman and a Christion, my experience has been a reliance on God in ways that have been unique to those two identifiers. Yes, we all need prayer, but given the traditionally unbalanced expectations of women, both in society and within our faith communities, many women will attest to how prayer has often served as a sanctuary of sort, where we are limitless in our ability to access the great equalizer, the one who came so that all might be free. In fact, the scripture teaches us in John 10:10 that the thief comes to steal, kill, and destroy, but Christ informs us that He came that we might have life more abundantly. In essence, what He was attempting to tell us is that when we are His, we have everything that we need and more. By being the sheep of his pasture, we are afforded the luxury of safety and well-being. Prayer is certainly a way to access the Father, our Protector, our Provider, our Source. In contemporary times, as women, there are those who seek to diminish our value, to take away our gifts and our talents, in fact, that is the job of the thief. But, as women and particularly as Christian women, we can hide in a place where no man, thief, or robber, can gain access to us. It is in our ability to pray that we find the much-needed liberation, freedom, and empowerment that God wants for us, all of us, including women. Therefore, if you are a woman who may love God, but struggle to converse with Him, perhaps as disciplined as you should, then this book is for you. And, in my observation of this fine work, even if you are not in relationship with God, but curious about a path to get to know who He is and how He works in the lives of others, this book is also for you. "Prayer the Supreme Weapon" will most certainly arm you with all the answers needed to begin, cultivate, and even affirm those strong prayer warriors, who have walked with God and served as prayer intercessors to address the needs of others as well as a dying world. My mother is a faithful prayer warrior, a woman whose entire life is a resounding testament to the power of prayer. A woman from humble beginnings whose life could have resulted in being the antithesis of how God has used and elevated her for such a time as this. In all honestly, her circumstances should not have rendered a women who became educated, an accomplished musician, vocalist, teacher, wife, mother, and spiritual leader, in her own right. And to this point, it should be noted that all leaders are not necessarily seen. Paradoxically, my mother's spiritual leadership has been one marked by being, instead, heard – and by a Higher Source. It has been her prayers that have sustained me, all of my siblings, her husband and their grandchildren, indeed, our entire family. As a prayer warrior, her "conversations" with God did not selfishly end with our home and family, but has extended to the countless women, children, and families she has also prayed for, and tirelessly. Please know, that such a leader exists inside all of us, and that leadership begins and ends with prayer.

INTRODUCTION

No weapon formed against me shall prosper!!!!

Weapons are used in many different forms in our world. Some ways we use weapons are for good, yet many more are used for evil. Webster's Dictionary describes a weapon as an instrument used in combat. Combat is to fight against or contend, which means to compete, struggle, or maintain. We can determine from these definitions that weapons were created to be used for protection as well as in the struggles of war, striving to bring about peace and claim ownership of territory. If we look at the way weapons are used today, protection and maintaining or conquering peace are the least explored areas of use.

The weapons of the current age have taken on different and multi-varied forms. There are all types of guns, knives, bombs, and even drugs that are included in the category of weapons. Their main purpose is not to protect, but to destroy, and bring about fear, violence, and death. We observe violence in our schools, churches, workplaces, and even recreational facilities.

How can we turn this negative impact on our society into a positive influence? Simply by implementing…

Prayer – The Supreme Weapon.

The world has just witnessed the turn of a century. We all excitedly waited for the clock to tick into the year Two

Thousand (2000). Millions of dollars were spent on celebrations. Many were fearful of the anticipated Y2K episode, so they purchased and stored an abundance of food and supplies. However, on the other hand, millions of sisters and brothers in Christ all over the world were praising God as we celebrated our own Y2K: "Saying Yes To the King." We used the most powerful weapon on earth, exercising our **Faith in God** through the power of **PRAYER**. By using this tool as our source of power, we entered the *New Millennium* without any fear. We know that by **Praising** and **Serving** the **Almighty King** we have been endowed with the greatest gift of all: **Prayer – The Supreme Weapon**.

This book has been written to provide Christian women, young and old, a guide to praying and staying connected to our heavenly Father. Regardless of where you are in your Christian walk, this guide can provide instruction and/or enhance your praying time and spiritual walk with God. So, let's get armed and dangerous as we enter into the various dimensions of prayer with **PRAYER – THE SUPREME WEAPON**.

CHAPTER ONE

WHAT IS PRAYER?

What is man that thou art mindful of him, for he was created in the likeness of God, a little lower than the angels. He is the apple of God's eye. Since woman was created from man, then she, too, is very special in the sight of God.

Now how does any of this relate to prayer?

Well, since we are made in the likeness of God, surely God would want us to keep a close relationship with him. As we know, one of the best ways to nurture any relationship is through communication. How do you suppose God intended for his people to connect to his power? Just as Daniel and Jesus did...through **PRAYER**.

> ***Prayer*** *is a conversation between God and his people.*
> *It is how we receive the power source to live.*

As no one can look upon the face of God, we must believe that when we talk to him, he will respond by answering our questions, giving directions for solving our problems, healing our sicknesses, and supplying all of our needs.

As we live our life on earth, we should strive to draw closer to God. I am reminded of the words of the hymn "O for a Closer Walk With God."

O for a closer walk with God,
A calm and Heavn'ly frame,
A light to shine upon the road
That leads me to the Lamb.

Where is the blessedness I knew,
When first I saw the Lord?
Where is the soul-refreshing view
Of Jesus and his love?

Prayer is the force that bonds us with God. As we continue to call upon him, he draws us to his power through prayer.

To pray is to talk aloud or silently to God.

CHAPTER TWO

HOW DO WE PRAY?

Jesus left us an example of how to pray in the 6th chapter of Matthew.

And when thou prayest, thou shalt not be as the hypocrites are: for they love to pray standing in the synagogues and in the corners of the streets, that they may be seen of men. Verily I say unto you, they have their reward. But thou, when thou prayest, enter into thy closet, and when thou hast shut thy door, pray to thy Father which is in secret; and thy Father which seeth in secret shall reward thee openly. But when ye pray, use not vain repetitions, as the heathen do: for they think that they shall be heard for their much speaking. Be not ye therefore like unto them; for your Father knoweth what things ye have need of, before ye ask him. After this manner therefore pray ye: Our Father which art in heaven, Hallowed be thy name. Thy kingdom come. Thy will be done in earth, as it is in heaven. Give us this day our daily bread. And forgive us our debts, as we forgive our debtors. And lead us not into temptation, but deliver us from evil: For thine is the kingdom, and the power, and the glory, forever. Amen. **Matthew 6:5-13**

The Five Steps to Prayer

STEP 1:   We must acknowledge our creator.
Our Father which art in Heaven…

STEP 2: We must cleanse ourselves by asking for forgiveness of our sins and the forgiveness of others whom we have wronged or who have wronged us.
Forgive us our debts, as we forgive our debtors...

STEP 3: We can then make our request to God.
Give us this day our daily bread.

STEP 4: We acknowledge the mighty power of God.
For Thine is the Kingdom and the power and the glory...

STEP 5: We acknowledge the timeless power of God and proclaim our thanks.
Forever...Amen.

If we follow God's example, we will truly be able to connect to his everlasting Power.

CHAPTER THREE

THE SIX METHODS OF PRAYER

The following methods are taken from "What Happens When Women Pray" by Evelyn Christenson.

Author Evelyn Christenson refers to the following methods of prayer as the Six S's. The S's cover every aspect or form of prayer. Through the use of these methods, one can advance from the shy, early beginner to a more established and strong prayer warrior.

1. Subject By Subject
The first "S" is Subject By Subject – praying in one accord about one subject at a time. As one person prays out loud, the rest pray silently on the same subject, not planning their own prayers in advance. This assures complete concentration and fervent prayer on one request at a time.

2. Short Prayers
Short Prayers, the second handle, are the secret of the success of small group prayer. Just one, or only a few sentences from each person on each subject allows time for all to pray if they wish. No one should be forced to pray aloud; let prayer be spontaneous, something a person wants to do, even if it's only to hear her own voice in prayer.

3. Simple Prayers

The third "S" is <u>Simple Prayers</u>. Those who have never prayed before will find it possible to utter one *simple* sentence from the heart when the leaders and other participants avoid using complicated phrases and a special prayer vocabulary.

4. Specific Prayer Requests

<u>Specific Requests</u> listed, and specific answers noted, are a great encouragement to continuing and expanded prayer. Use a notebook to list your requests and answers.

5. Silent Periods

The fifth "S" is <u>Silent Periods</u>. Silent Periods between prayers are a privilege and a blessing. Don't panic when there's a lull...just listen. Prayer is a two-way conversation with God.

6. Small Groups

<u>Small Groups</u>, the sixth "S", are usually best for newcomers, as well as for the shy or untrained. For some, it would take great courage to stand before hundreds of people and raise their voices in prayer for the first time. But in smaller groups, they can gain confidence in praying audibly.

The methods described in this chapter have been used by Evelyn Christenson in seminars repeatedly and have proven to be very successful.

CHAPTER FOUR

WOMEN OF THE BIBLE: EXAMPLES OF PRAYER

Throughout the Bible, there are women whose struggles were insurmountable. As we know, women had to follow certain customs. These included not being allowed in the temple at certain times of the month and covering their heads and faces while in public. As these women faced many problems of their era, their greatest source of power was through the intervention of God. This power was illustrated through prayer. I've looked at a few of these women, beginning with my favorite, Hannah.

HANNAH

When one thinks of praying women, Hannah always comes to mind. As is the story in the life of so many Bible women, her married life was shared with other women. Hannah was the first wife of Elkanah. Although she was reassured that her husband's love for her was genuine, the fact that she was barren and her husband's second wife had given him many children really troubled her. So often, when women are hurt or abused by other women, intentionally or unintentionally, they respond in a revengeful manner. However, Hannah carried all of her sorrow and hurt to God. Being fruitful (bearing children) was very important to women of the Bible times. Hannah harbored all of her pain, hurt, and despair in her heart.

Every year Hannah's family traveled from Ramah to Shilop to worship at the tabernacle. It was here that Hannah cried out and prayed in silence to the Lord to open her womb and give her a child and she would give it back to him.

God answered Hannah's prayer and gave her <u>Samuel</u>.

As God kept his promise, Hannah also kept hers by taking Samuel back to the temple and giving him back to the Lord. It is said that each year Hannah presented Samuel with a little robe she had sewn. Each time they visited the temple, Eli, the high priest, blessed her husband Elkanah, saying:

"May the Lord give you children by this woman to take the place of the one she prayed for and gave to the Lord." **I Samuel 2:20**

Because of Hannah's faithfulness, she became the mother of three sons and two daughters.

Isn't God *AWESOME*!

JEHOSHEBA

Jehosheba is considered a minor character in the Bible; however, her actions preserved the line of Judah from which the Messiah would come. She saved the life of her brother's youngest son, Joash, so that he would eventually become the rightful King of Judah.

Jehosheba was the wife of the priest Jehoiada, and the sister of Ahaziah. Jehosheba hid her brother's son Joash from the evil queen Athaliah (the daughter of Jezebel), whose plan was to kill him (2 Chronicles 22:11). Due to the brave actions of Jehosheba, Joash later became the King of Judah.

Sometimes our struggles are ways that God uses us to fulfill his promise, as was evident with Jehosheba. It was through her actions that God's promise of a Messiah from David's line, in the tribe of Judah, was manifested. Here we see one of the greatest prophecies fulfilled.

Jehosheba's prayer was one of guidance from God.

ELIZABETH

Elizabeth is known for being the mother of the forerunner of Jesus. It was in her womb that the baby leaped when she was visited by Mary, the mother of Jesus. She was considered a righteous woman, one who followed God's laws. If we are patient and wait on God, he will use us for some of his special tasks. Such was the case with Elizabeth.

Zechariah, Elizabeth's husband, was chosen to burn incense before the most holy place in the temple of the Lord. This was a great honor, one that Zechariah would never forget. It was during this ceremony that an angel appeared and told Zechariah that his wife would bear him a son. Because of Zechariah's age, he shouted in disbelief and was stricken with an inability to speak until the child was born.

The magnificence of God's power is tremendous as to how he can take a barren woman of age and give her a gift of life. Elizabeth later gave birth to John the Baptist, better known as the forerunner of Christ.

Elizabeth's prayer was one of thanksgiving for being chosen as such a vital servant of God.

MARY, THE MOTHER OF JESUS

We have given examples of various women of the Bible who were willing to step out in faith for innocent people, regardless of the consequences. One of the most forceful stories of the power of God is found in the story of the blessed mother of Jesus.

Here we find a very young girl in the prime of her life, about to be married to a decent man of society. This young virgin is faced with a gigantic situation that could bring her shame and cause her to lose her future husband. Mary stepped out on faith when she believed the angel who appeared and gave her the news that she would become pregnant and would give birth to Jesus. Mary humbly accepted the task before her. She, in her excitement, rushed to share this wonderful news with Elizabeth. This is the time when John the Baptist leaped in his mother Elizabeth's womb as Mary entered the door of their home. As Mary was much younger than her cousin Elizabeth, she stayed and cared for her cousin until John the Baptist was born.

Mary is a true example that nothing is impossible with God.

Mary's prayer is one of honor and thankfulness for being chosen as the most *BLESSED* mother of our Savior, Jesus.

CHAPTER FIVE

WHEN YOU CAN'T PRAY

Pray in the Time of Peace...

There will come a time, as it does in everyone's life, when you feel prayer is of no avail. You may have been praying for something special, over and over. However, it seems the more you pray the worse the circumstances become. There will be that instance when you don't know what to say or how to say it; when you feel that your conversation with God has concluded; when the words cannot be found to express your true feeling. It is at this time that Satan will try to shake the very grounds of your salvation. You may be claiming the salvation of your children, the happiness and peace of your family, the stability of your marriage—I could go on listing other circumstances. As I sit here at 4:00 a.m., I feel like Paul did in prison:

In whatsoever state I am, I will praise God.

What do you do when you can't pray? Stop, look around, and listen to God speaking to you. No matter how Satan is trying to rock my boat—which at this time I feel is torn into pieces, and I see no resolution to this storm in my life—just what is God saying to me? He's saying...Stand, stand, stand; be still, be still, be still. I will deliver you. Do not be shaken from your foundation. I see your pain, anguish, and hurt, but I can heal all of your wounds. I can lift you up. You must believe in my promise: I am with you.

It is at these times that we go to the E-M-R-S: Emergency-Meditation-(by)-Referencing-(the)-Source.

Some of which may sound something like…
Help me, Lord!
Lord, have mercy…I know you're there!
I praise you, Lord!
Lift me up, Lord!
And…Lord, you know!

You must always remember God's power is everlasting. If he could deliver Daniel by locking the jowls of the lion in the lion's den, then he can surely deliver us. When you cannot pray and Satan is about to devour your FAITH, look up and send PRAISES up to God. He will SUSTAIN and COMFORT you.

CHAPTER SIX

I'M STANDING ON THE PROMISES OF GOD

So he said, "I will certainly be with you..." **Exodus 3:12**

In the previous chapter, we talked about what to do when you can't pray. After experiencing the challenge of not being able to pray, I had to call in my prayer warriors to pray on my behalf. There will come a time in your life when you have to depend on other saints to intercede on your behalf. It is at this time, also, that Jesus and the Holy Spirit are powerful interceders to God. It is at this time that grace and mercy are utilized on our behalf. Therefore, we must be very careful of how we live and serve God, for God will remember and reward us justly.

There are many, many promises God has for us in his word. We could start in Genesis and go on through Revelation citing promise after promise, some even extending unto our time after death. Furthermore, after citing many promises, we could also find time and time again where God kept these promises. If this is true, and we proclaim it is, why do we find ourselves in situations where we can't hold a conversation with God? Because Satan is very much alive and he knows the address of every Christian. Not only does he know our address, but he has a master key...and he will come in.

I have just witnessed the most awesome power of God and intercessory prayer. As I arose this certain Sunday morning not knowing what the day would bring, Satan tried to deter me from attending service this day. Thinking of the goodness of God to me, I had decided to go ahead. Before departing, I chatted with one of my prayer warriors and the last statement I made before ending the conversation was "I'm going...*standing on the promises of God*."

As I went about my daily first Sunday tasks, I kept repeating in my mind some phrases from my EMRS. The service was progressing well and the time had come for the sermon. As the pastor took his text from Exodus 3:12, I thought his title would be *"Certainly I Will Be With You."* However, to my astonishment, the pastor's topic was **I'm Standing on the Promises of God**. *I was so amazed!* I just sat there and broke into tears. God gave me a profound confirmation of the promise...**I will be with you in the midst of your storm.**

To you who may be sinking in despair, it is true that if you just stand still, KEEPING the FAITH that God will keep his promise, you can truly be delivered through **PRAYER.**

CHAPTER SEVEN

GOD ALWAYS ANSWERS PRAYER

Ask, and it shall be given you; seek, and ye shall find; knock, and it shall be opened unto you; for everyone that asketh receiveth; and he that seeketh findeth; and to him that knocketh it shall be opened. **Matthew 7:7-8**

These words were spoken by Jesus and are considered just a few of the many promises made by him. The promises of God are not only true but must be fulfilled. This is the Christian's guarantee of our salvation, that if we trust and believe in God, we are saved and become inheritors of his promises. If you explore the Bible, you will find example after example where God kept his promise of deliverance whether it was for good fortune or for punishment for not obeying his will. He is truly a **man of his word**.

With this confirmation in mind, why do we sometimes doubt that God will answer our prayer? Simply because we refuse to accept the fact that answers come in different forms. We are always looking for him to answer *YES*; however, since God can see our future and knows exactly what we need, he can answer as he chooses. Sometimes, he says...*YES!...RIGHT NOW!* Other times, the answer may be...*MAYBE...I'LL SEE.* Another answer may be...*YES, BUT NOT NOW.* The answer that most Christians have problems with is when he says...<u>*NO!*</u>

I am reminded of the hardest time in my life when God's answer was...*NO*. It occurred about four years ago when I encountered a traumatic experience concerning our church minister of music, my brother in Christ, my prayer partner, and my surrogate brother. I felt, at that time, that God had given me a replacement for a very dear biological brother I had lost a few years before to cancer. I had watched my partner grow in his music ministry from the local to the national level. Thus, he grew closer to Christ. So much so, that some of his last words to me were "Rene, our people need to stop playing with God, for our time is short and I am ready." Little did I know at that time that this prophecy was about to take place.

As I left youth choir rehearsal the second Saturday in January, I was all excited to return on Sunday to tell him of an arrangement for us to coordinate a music workshop. Upon returning, I received the news that he had suffered what was thought to be a heart attack. Our church family, ministers, and friends rushed to the hospital. Churches and saints all over the country were praying and proclaiming that God would surely raise him up. We visited day and night, playing music, holding his hand, and doing everything we could think of to bring our friend and brother back. You would think that if two or three in one accord had power, what about thousands?

On Sunday at the beginning of our church worship, we received our answer...and it was **_NO_**. My friend had been taken home to play his music in Heaven and sing with the angels. **God Always Answers Prayer!**

CHAPTER EIGHT

HOW DO WE WAIT?

I waited patiently for the Lord and he inclined unto me, and heard my cry. **Psalm 40:1**

There is no doubt that if we make a request unto God, he will hear and answer our call. When the answer comes right away, we are grateful and filled with joy. Even when our answers come in just a little while, we are overwhelmed and thankful. But how does a Christian respond when God says...*LATER*? It is after many, many hours of praying, fasting, and meditation that we sometimes become weary; when it seems all of our service, suffering, and prayers have been in vain.

Hast thou not known? Hast thou not heard, that the everlasting God, the Lord, the creator of the ends of the earth, fainteth not, neither is weary? There is no searching of his understanding. He giveth power to the faint; and to them that have no might he increaseth strength. Even the youths shall faint and be weary and the young men shall utterly fall: <u>but they that wait upon the Lord shall renew their strength</u>; they shall mount up as eagles; they shall run and not be weary; and they shall walk and not faint. **Isaiah 40:28-31**

This scripture should be the preface with which we wait. God has assured us that if we trust and wait on him, he will deliver us. With this in mind, why do we find it hard to wait? Simply because we are flesh and Satan attacks our flesh during our weakest moments. It is at this time that our minds may wonder...*I've served you, God; fasted and prayed, and yet you refused to answer me.* Have you ever felt this way? Well, I have...and it was at my lowest point that Jesus spoke to me through a sermon or song.

I can remember being in that state of mind when I attended a funeral. Instead of only the family being lifted, I left that service thanking God for using me to suffer for him. It was after the service that I received a peace about all of my troubles. Oh, yes, I was still waiting, I was still hurting, and even still being mentally abused...but now, there was a **difference**. In fact, I could even reach out and help other sisters in my presence. God had shown me that my waiting was not in vain. He showed me that although, as a *Father*, he had refused to remove the cup from his son Jesus when he prayed in the Garden of Gethsemane, he delivered him later in a higher form. He gave him life over death.

That is what God will do for us in our waiting. He will lift us up, high as eagles, and carry us to heights beyond our imagination. He has the answer to fill your waiting hours.

Five Steps to Successful Waiting

STEP 1:   Pray and give your request to God.
  ***Blessed be God which hath not turned away my prayer, nor his mercy from me.* Psalm 66:20**

STEP 2:   There are times when we need to show we really believe God will answer our prayer by making a sacrifice through fasting.

33

And Jesus said unto them, Because of your unbelief: for verily I say unto you, if ye have faith as a grain of mustard seed, ye shall say unto this mountain, remove hence to yonder place: and it shall remove; and nothing shall be impossible unto you. Howbeit this kind goeth not out but by prayer and fasting. Matthew 17:20-21

STEP 3: We must study and read God's word. It is through his word that we gain strength. God will direct and lead you to the correct scripture to read. Fight Satan with the word of God. *Study to show thyself approved unto God, a workman that needeth not to be ashamed, rightly dividing the word of truth.* II Timothy 2:15

STEP 4: Praise him. We must praise him in worship. Peace and joy come from worshiping God. *O come, let us worship and bow down; let us kneel before the Lord our maker, for he is our God; and we are the people of his pasture and the sheep of his hand.* Psalm 95:6.

STEP 5: Give service. We should praise God in service, such as mission work, spiritual counseling, and helping the homeless and orphans. When we render service to others, God will surely reward us and give us peace. *In God have I put my trust: I will not be afraid what man can do unto me. Thy vows are upon me, O God: I will render praises unto thee.* Psalm 56:11-12

CHAPTER NINE

FAITH IS THE KEY

For we through the Spirit wait for the hope of righteousness by faith. **Galatians 5:5**

Faith is the substance of things hoped for and the evidence of things not seen. **Hebrews 11:1**

When we enter into a prayer covenant with God, we are seeking things we cannot see. We have numerous examples of instances where God has delivered; yet, until there is evidence of deliverance, we have to focus on the substance. We have hope of this substance in his word.

Be careful for nothing; but in every thing by prayer and supplication with thanksgiving, let your request be made known unto God. **Philippians 4:6**

Once our request has been made, we start looking for the evidence of deliverance. How do we look? We look with faith, believing that God will keep his promise. It doesn't matter how tough it gets, **we look**. Even when it appears as if our requests of faith will not come into fruition, **we look**. We look through heartaches, pain, suffering, despair, and sometimes...even joy. Nevertheless, **we never cease to look**. The woman with the issue of blood **looked** until she saw Jesus. She kept looking until she got close enough to touch the hem of his garment. She was healed and made whole.

There is a story I received in an email that I would like to share with you:

You Are My Sunshine

It is told that a young mother named Karen, after finding out she was going to have another baby, did what she could to help her 3-year-old son, Michael, prepare for a new sibling. They found out that the new baby was going to be a girl, and day after day, night after night, Michael would sing to his sister in his Mommy's tummy. He was building a bond of love with his little sister even before he met her.

The pregnancy progressed normally for Karen, who was an active member of her church. In time, the labor pains came, but serious complications arose during delivery and Karen had to have a C-section. After a long struggle, Michael's little sister was born, but she was in a very serious condition. The infant had to be rushed to the intensive care unit of a hospital in a nearby city.

As the days passed, the girl grew worse, and the doctor told the parents, "There is little hope. Be prepared for the worst." Karen and her husband were preparing for a funeral instead of fixing up the little room they had planned for her. However, her son kept begging, "I want to sing to her."

After two weeks, it seemed the funeral would come first. But Michael kept insisting, "Let me sing to her." After much thought, the mother decided to disregard the hospital rules. She dressed her son in an oversized scrub suit and marched with him into the ICU. After a consultation with the head nurse, Karen declared that her *son would not be leaving until he sang to his sister. As Michael gazed at the tiny infant losing the battle to live, in the voice of a 3-year-old he began to sing: "<u>You are my sunshine, my only sunshine, you make me happy when skies are gray.</u>"*

Instantly the baby girl seemed to respond. Her pulse rate began to calm down and become steady. "Keep on singing," encouraged Karen, with tears in her eyes. Michael sang "<u>You'll never know, dear, how much I love you; please don't take my sunshine away. The other night, dear, as I lay sleeping, I dreamed I held you in my arms</u>..." Michael's little sister began to relax, and healing seemed to sweep over her.

The next day—the very next day—the little girl was well enough to go home. Women's Day magazine called it <u>The Miracle of a Brother's Song</u>. The medical staff just called it a miracle. Karen called it a miracle of God's love.

This mother and son looked until her daughter and his sister gained life. As we trust in God and seek his deliverance by waiting in **faith**, we will find that the most trying times in our life...<u>are our most fruitful ones</u>.

Without faith, it is impossible to please God; he that cometh to God must believe that he is, and that he is a rewarder of them that diligently seek him. Hebrews 11:6

FAITH IS THE KEY TO ANSWERED PRAYER.

CHAPTER TEN

UNTIL THEN

And God shall wipe away all tears from their eyes; and there shall be no more death, neither sorrow, nor crying, neither shall there be any more pain: for the former things are passed away. **Revelation 21:4**

As we pray, wait, and struggle through the trials of this life, we find that God keeps all of his promises. As we go from day to day, we meet all kinds of challenges, which bring us to our knees. You may be a single parent trying to raise your child alone. You may be a husband or wife who has been hurt by your mate through mental abuse, ill compassion, or financial neglect. You may be a son or daughter who is in search of the joy and peace of God. You may be seeking stability or mental maturity. You may be that church member who is not following the will of God in your life, or one who is being attacked by Satan so much that you can't fully yield unto God. Then again, maybe you are that teenage girl or boy tangled in the decisions and fears of getting an education or staying sexually pure and free of drugs and alcohol usage. Maybe you are in a circumstance where you just don't know where to go or what to do.

If you find yourself in any of these situations, remember that God is always in control. He sends us his rainbow through the clouds as his assurance that his promise is true. We shall be delivered from all of our troubles.

Although sometimes we have a long, long wait, there is a rainbow in the midst of the clouds. Keep the faith; do not be overcome with the tricks of Satan. **God has all power**.

Somewhere over the rainbow, skies are blue. Somewhere over the rainbow, God will wipe all our tears away. Somewhere over the rainbow is a land that is fairer than day. As Jesus said...

Let not your heart be troubled: ye believe in God, believe also in me. In my Father's house are many mansions; if it were not so, I would have told you. I go to prepare a place for you. And if I go and prepare a place for you, I will come again, and receive you unto myself; that where I am, there ye may be also. **John 14:1-3**

<u>**Hold on, saints; hold on, children; hold on, mothers and fathers; hold on, sisters and brothers!!!**</u>

As it is written: *Eye hath not seen, nor ear heard, neither have entered into the heart of man, the things God hath prepared for them that love him.* **I Corinthians 2:9**

Until then...

P.U.S.H.

P-RAY

U-NTIL

S-OMETHING

H-APPENS

*We have God's
promise!*

He is the Promise Keeper and the Rainbow Giver!!

INSPIRATIONAL
THOUGHTS ON PRAYER

A Mother's Prayer for Guidance

Lord, you know we prayed for our children, and in your goodness, you gave us two. The first time we held them at birth, we could feel that you would protect them from danger, betrayal, and hurt.

Now, as a mother of young adults, I seek your strength in raising them in a world filled with no direction and ruins. Help me to keep strong guidance and loving thoughts, with you as our leader.

I pray for the rewards of this life, but I know there is a better life, where we will all meet someday.

Lord, I now understand the thanksgiving for the joys in this world; but I pray my children will always remember there is only one God, who art in heaven. One who cares and protects them even when parents are asleep.

Finally, Lord, if they stray from the values we have instilled, I pray that you come into their hearts to guide and help them make wise decisions, using good judgment and a desire for honorable work.

Thank you, Lord, for all the blessings you have bestowed upon us as a family.

Joe Ann Emanuel Deas

The Serenity Prayer

God grant me the serenity to
accept the things I cannot change;
courage to change the things I can;
and wisdom to know the difference.

Living one day at a time;
enjoying one moment at a time;
accepting hardships as the pathway to peace;
taking, as Jesus did, this sinful world
as it is, not as I would have it;
trusting that he will make all things right
if I surrender to his will,
that I may be reasonably happy in this life
and supremely happy with him
forever in the next.

Amen.

Reinhold Neibuhr

REFERENCES &
ILLUSTRATIONS

References

Christenson, Evelyn. (1975, 1991). *What Happens When Women Pray*. Chariot Victor Publishing, Colorado Springs, Colorado.

Deas, Joe Ann Emanuel. *"A Mother's Prayer for Guidance."* Used by permission.

Neibuhr, Reinhold. *"The Serenity Prayer."*

Spangler, Ann and Syswerda, Jean E. (1999). *Women of the Bible*. Zondervan Publishing House, Grand Rapids, Michigan.

The Holy Bible, King James Version. (1970). The National Bible Press, Philadelphia, Pennsylvania.

Illustrations

Front: Quinton Smith

Back: Kendal Smith

Printed in the United States
by Baker & Taylor Publisher Services